Lessons from Amy

Lessons from Amy

A devotional
to encourage
mothers of
special needs
children

Dora Wilbur

Carpenter's Son Publishing

Published by Carpenter's Son Publishing, Franklin,
Tennessee

Published in association with Larry Carpenter of Christian
Book Services, LLC

www.christianbookservices.com

Scripture quotations are taken from the Holy Bible,
New Living Translation, copyright ©1996, 2004, 2007,
by Tyndale House Foundation. Used by permission of
Tyndale House Publishers, Inc., Carol Stream, Illinois
60188. All rights reserved.

Scripture taken from THE HOLY BIBLE, NEW
INTERNATIONAL VERSION®, NIV® Copyright
© 1973, 1978, 1984, 2011 by Biblica, Inc.™ Used by
permission. All rights reserved worldwide.

Cover and Interior Design by Adept Content Solutions

Printed in the United States of America

978-1-952025-06-8

Contents

In Dedication

*Sometimes people come into your life for
a moment, a day, or a lifetime. It matters
not the time they spent with you but how
they impacted your life in that time.*
(Anonymous)

*Who would have dreamed a little girl with Down's
syndrome could change the lives of everyone she met?
Amy lived only ten short years on this earth, but her
memory and impact live on. The lessons learned from
her are endless. This book chronicles Amy's gentle nature
and how she transformed the lives of her family and
friends. The story is told through the eyes of her mother
Lois. May it bring you encouragement and hope as
you raise a special needs child. Just as Amy is sheltered
in the arms of her heavenly Father, may you know He
is faithfully and continually watching over you.*

Trust

Every good and perfect gift is from above, coming down from the Father of the heavenly lights. (James 1:17, NIV)

There are mornings when you wake up and there's nothing to indicate that your life is about to change. That's what happened the day Amy was born. Bob and I went to the hospital as we had with our three other children. However, when the baby came this time, the doctor turned quickly away from me. I didn't even see her. I sensed something was wrong but didn't know what it could be. One thing was glaring; there was no sound coming from my baby, not even a whimper. The doctor just turned and walked out of the room with Amy.

I was left alone in total confusion. What was happening? The nurse informed me Amy was on a respirator because she was having trouble breathing. She said the doctor would be in to talk to us. The doctor told Bob our baby probably wouldn't survive long. The doctor said, "Your baby is mongoloid." That was his word for "mentally retarded," (presently referred to as Down's syndrome). He suggested we leave her at the hospital, thinking she would only live a few days. Bob and I disagreed. She was our little girl, and we were absolutely keeping her. Amy was our special gift.

> *How many of us have questioned our circumstances? Maybe we've even questioned God. It's easy to do when we are confused, scared, or hurt. But God wants us to trust Him. "Trust in the LORD with all your heart and lean not on your own understanding; in all your ways submit to him, and he will make your paths straight." (Proverbs 3:5–6 NIV) Sometimes what we see in front of us doesn't seem to make any sense, but we need to remember God has a good plan for our lives and our lives are still in process.*

Perhaps you went to the hospital expecting to take home a healthy baby, but instead you have a baby who is facing insurmountable challenges. Take a deep breath and lean into the God who is forever watching over you and your little one. You can most certainly say, "When I am afraid, I put my trust in you." (Psalm 56:3, NIV).

This road called life takes many twists and turns. Trust God with the details.

My prayer for today...

_____

_____

_____

_____

_____

_____

_____

_____

_____

_____

Wisdom

Blessed are those who find wisdom,
those who gain understanding.
(Proverbs 3:13, NIV)

Sometimes when you are facing a new situation, questions arise that you can't answer. When we brought Amy home from the hospital, this was true for us. She had a hole in her heart and a high risk for infection. How could we protect a child from the germs in the air, let alone those on the farm where we were living? Bob and I needed a place where we could keep Amy as safe as possible, but we had no idea how to accomplish that. Eventually, we decided the small den off the main living room could be transformed and made into a nursery. This allowed me to stay with Amy continually, even sleeping on a small sofa in the room.

We had many family and friends who wanted to see and meet Amy. However, every single one of them carried microorganisms that could be fatal to her, especially in those early days. After careful thought, we came up with a workable solution. When visitors stopped by, we'd have them come around to the side of the house that had a window looking into the den. Then, I'd hold Amy up to the window and our friends and family could see our beautiful daughter. It was a bit unorthodox, but it worked to protect our little baby.

Throughout the day, we are constantly making critical decisions. Wisdom can be hard to come by, but we don't have to make decisions alone! We can ask God for help. "If any of you lacks wisdom, you should ask God, who gives generously to all without finding fault, and it will be given to you." (James 1:5, NIV). God is full of knowledge and understanding, and He knows just how to help in your unique circumstances.

Lessons from Amy

The special needs of your child can be over-whelming if you don't know what to do. Relax; no one expects you to have all the answers. God stands ready and He willingly gives guidance in your moments of uncertainty. "God is our refuge and strength, an ever-present help in trouble." (Psalm 46:1, NIV).

It's impossible to know exactly what to do in every situation. Ask God for wisdom.

My prayer for today...

Help

The righteous cry out, and the LORD hears them; he delivers them from all their troubles. (Psalm 34:17 NIV)

I learned to handle emergencies right away. Early one morning when Amy was just two months old, she began to hiccup and then struggle for breath. It wasn't long before she began to turn blue. Bob was in the field, so our son Don ran to get him. I grabbed a blanket from the couch for Amy, and off we went. With no 911 at the time, we had to rush to the doctor ourselves. The doctor's office was packed when we arrived, but an alert nurse grabbed my arm and led us quickly back to the doctor.

The doctor immediately gave Amy oxygen, then called an ambulance himself. He explained that Amy's airway was blocked and told us exactly what was going to be needed when she arrived at the hospital. To my surprise, when the ambulance arrived the doctor took Amy and climbed in. The hole in Amy's heart was life-threatening. They unblocked the airway and sent her to Cleveland Clinic for a heart catheter. That's when they learned she had four holes in her heart. Despite this, we were still able to bring our baby home the day before Thanksgiving.

A crisis is always unexpected. When we feel powerless, we're not sure what to do. But we never have to face any crisis alone. "So do not fear, for I am with you; do not be dismayed, for I am your God. I will strengthen you and help you; I will uphold you with my righteous right hand." (Isaiah 41:10, NIV). God wants to help you in every situation you face. Call on Him in your times of trouble, and He will come running to give you the help you need.

You may find yourself in the middle of a challenge too big for you. You may not know what to do for your child or who to turn to for the help you need. Don't go it alone—go to the One who has all the answers and can guide you down the right path. Stand on this promise, "My help comes from the LORD, the Maker of heaven and earth." (Psalm 121:2, NIV). God doesn't want you to face any trial alone. He loves you. He loves your child. It's as simple as that.

Your life may be filled with too many questions and not enough answers. Call on the One who has all the solutions.

My prayer for today...

_____

_____

_____

_____

_____

_____

_____

_____

Direction

The LORD himself goes before you and will be with you; he will never leave you nor forsake you. Do not be afraid; do not be discouraged. (Deuteronomy 31:8, NIV)

Have you ever been in the middle of a situation when you couldn't see the forest for the trees? That happened to me at Christmastime when Amy was one year old and in the hospital. I stayed in her room constantly; my entire being focused on her recovery. Amy was on oxygen, so I sat near her bed and refused to leave her side. As hospital workers came and went, my eyes stayed on Amy. I prayed continually for a change in her condition.

At some point, the doctor came and asked me if I still had Christmas shopping to do. It was such an odd question considering my little girl was in the hospital. He said, "You have three other kids at home, and they need your attention too." Surprisingly, the doctor promised to stay with Amy while I went shopping. I left immediately and quickly and easily found presents. When I returned, Amy was wiggling and looking around! The doctor said, "We had a good time while you were gone." While I was shopping, he removed Amy from the oxygen. She came home with me that night, and our Christmas was full of joy-filled blessings.

Getting caught up in a trying situation is easy to do. We tend to look at the one thing that is going wrong and miss the One who is always there guiding us. When you're feeling afraid, it's hard to think of anything else. It's good to remember: "I know the LORD is always with me. I will not be shaken, for He is right beside me." (Psalm 16:8, NLT). God is not going to leave you alone with your problem. He's going to be right there beside you, leading you back to solid ground.

If focusing every waking moment on the particular care of your child is making it hard to function, you can get help. God wants to be there for you. He wants to ease the burdens you are carrying. "Give all your worries and cares to God, for he cares about you." (1 Peter 5:7, NLT). You're not alone. God is standing at the ready to carry that heavy load for you. Won't you give it to Him?

If worry is taking over your life, hand it over to the One who created heaven and earth. After all, He's got the whole world in His hands.

My prayer for today...

_____

_____

_____

_____

_____

_____

_____

Togetherness

Live in harmony with each other.
(Romans 12:16, NIV)

A baby beautifully brings a family together. Although our lives were very busy on the farm, everyone took time to stop and visit with Amy. We placed her on the big couch in the living room propped up by a pillow. She was a quiet baby, never crying, and only occasionally making small gurgling noises. Amy couldn't turn her head from side to side, but she would look right into your eyes if you sat facing her. By sitting in front of her, our family brought her into our circle of love.

When Bob came in from his chores, he'd stop to chat with Amy. He liked to ask her questions. "How are you doing today?" "Are you having a good day?" "Are you happy?" That was his way of loving on his little girl. When I was holding Amy, the kids would come and talk to her. I would put my hand on the back of her head, and pretend Amy was saying yes or no when they asked her a question. The kids would get excited and yell, "She said yes!" With sweet and simple conversations, the whole family was able to interact with Amy.

God wants to have simple and easy conversations too. He invites us to come to Him in prayer. He wants to talk about all the big things in our lives; He wants to talk about all the little things too. "This is the confidence we have in approaching God: that if we ask anything according to his will, he hears us." (1 John 5:14, NIV) You probably have a million thoughts going through your mind each day, and it's good to know God is right there with you. He's a strong proponent of unity.

Your world can slow down when you have a child who needs your constant attention. However, it seems everyone around you is moving at a fast pace. When this happens, you can feel disconnected from the very people closest to you. You can even feel disconnected from God. Nevertheless, you need to realize that your emotions are causing you to feel lonely, and your emotions can distort the truth. The truth is, you are never alone; God is always with you. You can whisper a quiet prayer and He hears you. "The LORD is near to all who call on him, to all who call on him in truth." (Psalm 145:18, NIV). God loves togetherness and staying close to you is His favorite pastime.

You never have to face one moment alone. Invite God into your day.

My prayer for today...

_____

_____

_____

_____

_____

_____

Possibilities

With man this is impossible, but not with God; all things are possible with God. (Mark 10:27, NIV)

All children have unique challenges as they grow. Some have more challenges than others. That's what happened when Amy tried to learn to walk. Thinking that she could walk seemed outrageous when standing was causing her problems. It didn't help that the doctor's expectations were so low. He kept telling us she wouldn't learn to talk, and she certainly wouldn't learn to walk. The family, however, had other plans for Amy.

Don tried to help by putting Amy's feet on his and walking with her. Sometimes family members would get on either side of her to support and guide her along. One day, Amy started to waddle on her own. She'd stick her arms straight out for balance and make it about two steps before she plopped back down on her bottom. Eventually, she was able to add to the number of steps she could take. A year later, when the doctor saw Amy walking, he was amazed. God had the last word on that subject.

We can hear news from a professional that overwhelms us. We wonder how we are ever going to cope. But we must not give up! God is watching over us, and His thoughts are higher than our thoughts. He wants to change things in our favor. "But as for you, be strong and do not give up, for your work will be rewarded." (2 Chronicles 15:7, NIV). Even when things look bad, we can stand strong.

It's difficult to hear bad news about your child. Our instincts tell us to run and hide our child. We start to have a "me against the world" mentality. But you are not fighting any of your battles alone. "Do not be afraid of them; the LORD your God himself will fight for you." (Deuteronomy 3:22, NIV). God is fighting for your child, and He always wins the fight. "But thank God! He has made us his captives and continues to lead us along in Christ's triumphal procession. Now he uses us to spread the knowledge of Christ everywhere, like a sweet perfume." (2 Corinthians 2:14, NLT).

Fighting a battle today? Let God take the lead; He knows how to win the war.

My prayer for today...

_____

_____

_____

_____

_____

_____

_____

_____

_____

_____

_____

_____

Counsel

I will instruct you and teach you
in the way which you should go;
I will counsel you with my loving
eye on you. (Psalm 32:8, NIV)

There are days when life seems too much for us. We have so many things to do, an abundance of worries, and very little time to deal with them all. This happened to me during one of the many times Amy had to stay in the hospital. She was there because her breathing was labored. I was sitting alone in her room with too many thoughts when the doctor walked in and sat down. He realized I was on edge, and I think he wanted to stay and give me some comfort.

The doctor shared his thoughts. He said everyone has problems. Some may be bigger than others, but everyone has them. Since we don't know what the next minute holds, we must take it one day at a time. God agrees. "Therefore do not worry about tomorrow, for tomorrow will worry about itself. Each day has enough trouble of its own." (Matthew 6:34, NIV). The doctor said there will always be bumps in the road. We just need to choose how we will navigate them.

Life has a way of throwing us curveballs. We are expecting the day to go one way, but it takes a turn in a whole new direction. That's when we need guidance from someone a lot smarter than us. God knows exactly what to do in a crisis. "Whether you turn to the right or to the left, your ears will hear a voice behind you, saying, 'This is the way; walk in it.'" (Isaiah 30:21, NIV). When we're not sure what the next moment holds, we can hold fast to the One who knows exactly what to do.

When you're raising a child with specific needs, you are constantly second-guessing your own decisions. Navigating new territory can be scary, but you can ask God for directions. You don't have to make one decision alone. Just ask: "Show me the right path, O LORD; point out the road for me to follow. Lead me by your truth and teach me, for you are the God who saves me. All day long I put my hope in you." (Psalm 25:4–5, NLT) God will help you make the best decisions for your child. Walk with Him; He'll take you down the right path.

Are you having troubled thoughts?
Call on the One who calms the sea.

My prayer for today...

Affection

*But you, O LORD, are a God of
compassion and mercy, slow to get angry
and filled with unfailing love and
faithfulness. (Psalm 86:15, NLT)*

Susan was a perfect big sister for Amy. She created simple games so Amy could have the most fun. In Susan's bedroom, they often played hide and seek. Although the hiding places were scarce, Amy would hide beside the bed, behind the curtains, or behind some clothes. Susan would play along and say, "Where's Amy? I can't find her." Amy would jump out and say "Boo!" every time.

Books were often a part of the playtime. Susan used these moments to try to teach Amy.

She'd say, "Go get the red book for us to read," or "Pick up the big book this time." Then they'd get on the bed and Susan would read to Amy. They also practiced coordination skills together. They would clap and do various hand gestures. Susan's affection for Amy showed in the time they spent together and in the way she was always trying to help her learn.

Sometimes the unfolding of our lives is difficult. That's when we need someone teaching us where to turn, what to do, or what to say. God has infinite wisdom to help us along. It's also abounding in extra benefits. "But the wisdom from above is first of all pure. It is also peace loving, gentle at all times, and willing to yield to others. It is full of mercy and the fruit of good deeds. It shows no favoritism and is always sincere." (James 3:17, NLT). Unfortunately, the storms of life will come, so pick up a heavy dose of God's wisdom to see you through.

There are days when it seems your child is facing insurmountable obstacles. You wonder if things will ever change. Despite the current circumstances, God's plan for your child is good. "'For I know the plans I have for you,' says the LORD. 'They are plans for good and not for disaster, to give you a future and a hope.'" (Jeremiah 29:11, NLT). He loves your child so much that He plans for beautiful days. He wants you to look with hope into your child's future. "He has made everything beautiful in its time." (Ecclesiastes 3:11a, NIV). God is planning special days for you and your child. His affection for you never ends.

When all is dark around you, look around and find God's light.

My prayer for today...

_____

_____

_____

_____

_____

_____

_____

_____

Attentiveness

The eyes of the LORD are on the righteous, and his ears are attentive to their cry. (Psalm 34:15, NIV)

Don and Bobby had a special relationship with Amy. Although they were older, they always took the time to give her some attention. They enjoyed giving her rides on a motor scooter. She loved sitting on her brothers' laps while zooming around the yard. They even tried to play kickball with her. She wasn't much for kicking, so she'd pick it up and set it down just to have them kick it all over again. They were so patient with her!

Amy preferred the outdoors, but sometimes the weather kept her inside. When this happened, she got the boys to watch cartoons with her. They'd all lie on the floor and watch Oscar the Grouch and laugh at the silly show. They even took the time to color in her coloring book with her. Amy loved spending time with her big brothers.

We can rest in the knowledge that God pays attention to us too. He is always listening. "I will answer them before they even call to me. While they are still talking about their needs, I will go ahead and answer their prayers!" (Isaiah 65:24, NLT). God isn't talking on His cell phone and not paying attention to our prayers. Because of His amazing love, He is totally focused on us. "The LORD appeared to us in the past, saying: 'I have loved you with an everlasting love; I have drawn you with unfailing kindness.'" (Jeremiah 31:3b, NIV).

Watching over your child is a full-time job, but who watches over you? Your heavenly Father's faithful attention never waivers. "He will not let your foot slip—he who watches over you will not slumber." (Psalm 121:3, NIV). When it seems you are alone and making hard decisions about your child's welfare, keep in mind you are never alone. God is interested in every detail of your life.

He wants to be there in the moments of celebration and when you are in the trenches. "When they call on me, I will answer; I will be with them in trouble. I will rescue and honor them. I will reward them with a long life and give them my salvation." (Psalm 91:15–16, NLT).

You are not fighting any battle alone. God is constantly standing with you.

My prayer for today...

_____

_____

_____

_____

_____

_____

_____

_____

_____

_____

Joy

This is the day the LORD has made. We will rejoice and be glad in it.
(Psalm 118:24, NLT)

It's easy to face each day with a list of things to do, but a child sees the world in a much different light. My family and I would visit a large community pool each summer. The lawn surrounding the pool was filled with blankets, beach towels, and people. They also had a snack bar that my kids loved to visit. One day we all walked over to get a cold pop. It was a crowded day, so I held fast to Amy's hand. Somehow, while we were waiting in line, deciding what we wanted and getting the money ready, Amy disappeared. It happened in the blink of an eye.

Everyone helped to look for her: my family, our friends, and total strangers who saw our distress. She was found by a friend, standing near a pond looking at the ducks. She was enthralled! Amy was talking to them, and her face held a beautiful smile. We were so thankful to find her quickly. My son Bobby went and took her hand, which she accepted gladly, happily moving towards her next adventure.

We tend to move through life with a mental "to do" list that is always too long. Sometimes we forget the joy in the little moments. Children never do; they are constantly seeking out fun things to do. Jesus didn't intend for us to live a life that follows a checklist. He said, "I have come that they may have life and have it to the full." (John 10:10, NIV). There are opportunities in each day to feel the goodness of God. We just need to hit the pause button long enough to experience them.

Taking care of a child who needs a lot of attention narrows your focus. When you feel yourself going through the motions of your day, pause.

God wants to fill you with joy in that moment. He knows if you will allow joy to come in, your strength will rise. When your strength rises, even all the cares of the world won't be able to stop you. Here's a secret worth sharing, "...the joy of the LORD is your strength." (Nehemiah 8:10, NIV).

There will always be a list of things to do. Do something today that brings you joy.

My prayer for today...

Compassion

Finally, all of you, be like-minded, be sympathetic, love one another, be compassionate and humble. (1 Peter 3:8, NIV)

Sometimes the lessons we learn come from unexpected places. One day while Bob was reading the paper and I was fixing supper, Amy caught our attention in a most unusual way. She was in her room quietly playing with the radio turned on. It was on a Christian radio station that the family enjoyed in the evenings. While I was cooking dinner, Bob cried out to me, "Lois, there's something wrong with Amy." Dropping everything, I hurried towards her room.

As I stood in the doorway and watched Amy, it took me a minute to realize what was going on. She had one hand on the top of the radio, and another held high in the air. Tears were streaming down her beautiful face, and she was mumbling along with the person on the radio. As I listened to the broadcast, I noticed they were praying for someone. That's when I knew Amy was praying in her own special way too, asking God to grant the prayer request. It was a simple plea, given out of compassion, and it went straight to the Father's heart.

We don't have to use big words and try to be formal when we talk to our heavenly Father. We just need to be sincere. He cares so much for us. God says, "For the eyes of the LORD are on the righteous and his ears are attentive to their prayer." (1 Peter 3:12a, NIV). He hears us. He listens to our cry for help. Sometimes we need prayer for several problems and we don't know where to begin. That's okay too. God can handle it all. In those desperate times, we can simply say, "Father, help me."

You have a child that has many needs. Talk to God about your fears; don't hesitate because

Lessons from Amy

you don't know what to say or how to ask. All His thoughts are loving towards you. "But you, LORD, are a compassionate and gracious God, slow to anger, abounding in love and faithfulness." (Psalm 86:15, NIV) You can trust God's love for you, and you can trust the boundless love of God for your child. It never waivers; it never ends.

Reach out to the Father today; He is expectantly waiting your call.

My prayer for today...

_____

_____

_____

_____

_____

_____

_____

_____

_____

_____

Delightful

"Do you hear what these children are saying?" they asked him. "Yes," replied Jesus, "have you never read, ""From the lips of children and infants you, Lord, have called forth your praise'?"(Matthew 21:16, NIV)

Hearing Amy sing and clap made me smile. She seemed to especially like singing in the car. One of her favorite songs had these lines, "Here's my cup Lord, fill it up Lord." Amy would cup her hands together and hold them high in the air for God to fill them up. My heart was touched in those moments, because I could see on her face the sincerity of her words. Having my faith grow because of a child's song was one of the many mysteries in the life of Amy. Although I've pondered how she did it, she seemed to have a way of constantly teaching me about a life well-lived.

She created her own songs too. These were very entertaining, as she included the names of family members and pets in them. She had many versions of "Jesus Loves Me." She would say "Jesus loves Mommy and Daddy, Jesus loves Don and Bobby, and Jesus even loves Sam and Barabbas." These were our family pets! Although I loved hearing our names, I must admit that animals of any kind usually took top billing. Amy loved all creatures great and small.

Music can soothe our souls and lift our spirits. Can you imagine that the Creator of the universe looks at us with such love that He must sing? "For the LORD your God is living among you. He is a mighty savior. He will take delight in you with gladness. With his love, he will calm all your fears. He will rejoice over you with joyful songs." (Zephaniah 3:17, NLT). Clearly, we are well loved.

It's probably hard to imagine that as you care for your child, God is watching over you with special care. You are the charming child in this picture. "The LORD watches over you—the LORD is your shade at your right hand; the sun will not harm you by day, nor the moon by night. The LORD will keep you from all harm—He will watch over your life; the LORD will watch over your coming and going both now and forevermore." (Psalm 121: 5–8, NIV). Just as you lovingly protect and care for your child, God is lovingly protecting you, and He chooses to sing with joy as He does it.

> *Look in the mirror and you'll*
> *see God's much-loved child.*

My prayer for today...

_____

_____

_____

_____

_____

_____

Gentleness

Let your gentleness be evident to all. The LORD is near. (Philippians 4:5, NIV)

Amy had a special way with animals. They seemed to know she was a safe place to land—often literally. Her brother Don got a dog from the neighbors and brought her home. Amy named him Puppy. When she clapped her hands, Puppy came running and jumped into her waiting arms. She loved to give the dog treats, which included any type of food that was in her hand. If she sat on the ground, Puppy climbed into her lap, and she put her arm around him. They were best buds.

At age seven, Amy was in the hospital right before Easter. Her sister Susan sneaked a rabbit into the room and told Amy it was the Easter

Bunny. She brought it in a shoebox, and Amy named it Bunny. It was quite tame and sat comfortably on Amy's lap. She was gently stroking him when the nurse came in and asked if everything was okay. We didn't know what we should say about the rabbit. Thankfully, the nurse just smiled and left without asking any more questions. When Susan left, Bunny went too, probably looking forward to Amy's homecoming.

God has a special way of handling us too. He knows we are dealing with a lot of challenges, so He is extra protective. God wants us to know we are safe with Him. "He will cover you with his feathers. He will shelter you with his wings. His faithful promises are your armor and protection." (Psalm 91:4, NLT). It's okay to lean on Him in trying times. It's okay to reach out your hand to take His. "For I am the LORD your God who takes hold of your right hand and says to you, do not fear; I will help you." (Isaiah 41:13, NIV)

When you're in the middle of a battle, it feels like you're in it alone. But that is not the case at all. God says, "Do not fear, for I have redeemed you; I have summoned you by name; you are mine. *When you pass through the waters, I will be with you; and when you pass through the rivers, they will not sweep over you. When you walk through the fire, you will not be burned; the flames will not set you ablaze." (Isaiah 43:1b-2, NIV). There are all kinds of storms coming at you when you're trying to shield and protect your child, but God is the One who can calm the storms around you. Trust in the promise of His care.*

Standing in a storm? Get under the protection of His umbrella today.

My prayer for today...

Acceptance

Accept one another, then, just as Christ accepted you, in order to bring praise to God. (Romans 15:7, NIV)

Treating others kindly was a way of life for Amy. She had a special way of seeing the world and all the people in it. Amy attended the School of Hope, where she was able to receive individual attention for her special needs. One year, I took Amy to meet her new teacher, who happened to be an African American man. A few days later we attended an open house for the school, which was held in their auditorium.

When we arrived at the open house, there were a few dozen people in the room. As we were looking around, I spotted Amy's teacher in the crowd. I said, "Look Amy, there's your new teacher." Amy kept saying, "Where? Where?" I was surprised that Amy didn't see him, because her teacher happened to be the only African American in the room that day. That's when I realized Amy didn't see people as black or white. She looked at people the way God does; she looked at their hearts.

Adults regularly judge people with their thoughts. We think, "She works hard, but that guy is lazy." Or, "He's so tall, but his friend is short." What does any of that even matter? We should look at people through God's eyes. "The LORD doesn't see things the way you see them. People judge by outward appearance, but the LORD looks at the heart." (1 Samuel 16:7, NLT). We need to see people through the lens of God's heart for them.

Sometimes you hear the people around you talking negatively. It especially hurts when you hear people say judgmental things about your child. You can ignore all that negativity because you know God understands what you're going through. "So be strong and courageous! Do not be afraid and do

Lessons from Amy

not panic before them. For the LORD your God will personally go ahead of you. He will neither fail you nor abandon you." (Deuteronomy 31:6, NLT). Have faith that God sees what you are going through and He will never leave your side.

Trust in this promise: Jesus has a big heart for little children.

My prayer for today...

_____

_____

_____

_____

_____

_____

_____

_____

_____

_____

Friendship

*Do to others as you would have them
do to you. (Luke 6:31, NIV)*

Amy was always a ray of sunshine wherever we
went. When we went shopping, she said "Hi!" to
everyone we passed. They couldn't help but smile
and return her greeting. If we were in line at the
grocery store to pay, she would turn around and
look at the person behind us. When Amy caught
their attention, she would give them a friendly
little wave. Family members received a warm
hug along with their greeting. Amy loved well.

At school, Amy often thought of others
before herself. One day at lunch she had two
cookies and insisted on sharing one with a class-
mate. Another day Amy watched the girl next to

her eat peas one at a time. When the little girl's vegetables were gone, Amy decided to share. She took the peas off her own plate and slid them on her neighbor's plate. Amy had a generous heart.

It's easy to get caught up in our own little world and not notice the people around us. Lucky for us, that does not describe the Lord. His love for us is constant, and He wants that to be a way of life for us too. "This is my commandment: Love each other in the same way I have loved you." (John 15:12, NLT). Let's pay attention to the people around us, because we may be able to help in their time of need.

When you have a child who requires extra attention, often you could use some help. Your whole day is focused on your child, it's filled with constant movement, and it's overflowing with rushing thoughts. God wants to step into your day and give you the one thing that is extremely hard to find: peace. His peace is better than just a little bit of quiet. "Peace I leave with you; my peace I give you. I do not give to you as the world gives. Do not let your hearts be troubled and do not be afraid." (John 14:27, NIV). Understandably, you have anxious thoughts about your child's needs; but God says that you should not be afraid. He will stay close. "Surely your goodness and love will follow me all the days of my life, and I will dwell in the house of the LORD forever." (Psalm 23:6, NIV). He wants to help, and He will stay near as you care for your child.

Feeling a little lost today? Why not call Jesus? He knows how to be a good friend.

My prayer for today...

_____

_____

_____

_____

_____

_____

_____

_____

_____

Support

For he will deliver the needy who cry out, the afflicted who have no one to help. (Psalm 72:12, NIV)

Watching Amy interact with other children was humbling. She had a gentle way of helping kids in need. At the School of Hope, children frequently spilled their juice, dropped their toys, and stumbled as they walked along. At times, Amy noticed these things even before the adults could react. One day a child dropped his crayons, and they went under the table. Amy and the other children immediately crawled all around picking up the rolling crayons and bringing them to the boy.

Amy was able to help in other ways too. One child was unsuccessfully stacking building blocks. He tried to do it over and over as the blocks kept toppling over. When he finally got a few on top of each other, Amy clapped and smiled at his success. She had an exceptional way of celebrating the accomplishments of her classmates. She loved when other children succeeded, whether the task was great or small.

When we're stacking up the building blocks of our life, it can sometimes feel like those blocks are continually falling over. That's when we need to look to the heavens for our support. The Lord stands ready to help. "Surely God is my help; the LORD is the one who sustains me." (Psalm 54:4, NIV). The degree of challenge we face isn't an issue, for God wants us to continually succeed. He helps in the small difficulties and in the seemingly insurmountable ones too.

Some days, problems come from every direction. With your unique child, you may wonder, "Where should I start?" But you are determined and the Father is on your side, so you can face each challenge with confidence that it will be conquered.

"Because the Sovereign LORD helps me, I will not be disgraced. Therefore have I set my face like flint, and I know I will not be put to shame." (Isaiah 50:7, NIV). This current set of problems will not stop you. With God's help, you will stay strong.

With God by your side, you are sure to win every battle.

My prayer for today...

_____

_____

_____

_____

_____

_____

_____

_____

_____

_____

Kindness

Since God chose you to be the holy people he loves, you must clothe yourselves with tenderhearted mercy, kindness, humility, gentleness, and patience. (Colossians 3:12, NLT)

They say animals instinctively know whether they can trust people. Based on the many animals on our farm and the way they gravitated to Amy, I think it's true. Like so many farmers, we had barn cats. Amy went out to see them every day. Somehow, they knew when she was outside, because they ran straight for her. She would sit on the grass and pet each one. Our stray cats were well loved by Amy.

She loved all animals—including the cows! She headed straight for the barn when we were outside. She wanted to look in on the cattle and watch over them. If they were in the pasture, she'd go right to the edge of the field and stare at them. There was something in the way she watched them that let me know she was making sure they were okay.

Our instincts should tell us we can trust God too. He has all the qualities of a loving Father. "God's way is perfect. All the LORD's promises prove true. He is a shield for all who look to him for protection." (Psalm 18:30, NLT). He wants to be part of our everyday lives. He is like the little girl standing at the edge of the field watching over her cows. He is like an eagle watching over its babies. "Like an eagle that rouses her chicks and hovers over her young, so he spread his wings to take them up and carried them safely on his pinions." (Deuteronomy 32:11, NLT)

You watch over your child just as your Father watches over you. Your child is precious to you; and that's exactly how God feels about your child. Even on the tough days, if you keep trusting Him, you will stay strong. "But blessed are those who trust in the LORD and have made the LORD their hope and confidence. They are like trees planted along a riverbank, with roots that reach deep into the water. Such trees are not bothered by the heat or worried by long months of drought. Their leaves stay green, and they never stop producing fruit." (Jeremiah 17:7–8, NLT). You are safe with God.

Inside or outside, you can run to your Father's waiting arms.

My prayer for today...

Safekeeping

My God is my rock, in whom I take refuge, my shield and the horn of my salvation. He is my stronghold, my refuge and my savior. (2 Samuel 22:3, NIV)

We had a major scare when Amy was six years old. Susan had just gotten her driver's license and decided to take Amy for a ride around the block. Back then, no one wore seatbelts. They weren't even a mile down the road when Amy started touching the buttons on the passenger door. Susan reached over to grab Amy's hand and somehow abruptly turned the steering wheel at the same time. Unfortunately, the car careened into an abutment, smashing its entire front.

Poor Susan was covered in glass from the windshield. Looking over, she was confused to see Amy sitting on the ground. That's when she realized the front of the car was displaced into the backseat, including the floorboard! Strangely enough, it didn't take Amy with it. The neighbors called us and rushed the girls to the hospital. Susan had some minor cuts from the windshield. Amy had a scrape on her knee, which the doctor covered with a Band-Aid. Remarkably, even though the car was totaled, our girls were both okay.

We all have times when it feels like we've run into a brick wall. Unwanted news reaches us and knocks us to our knees. We get a bad result in a medical checkup. We have too many questions and not enough answers. That's when we need to know we are protected by a loving Father. "You have given me your shield of victory. Your right hand supports me; your help has made me great. You have made a wide path for my feet to keep them from slipping." (Psalm 18:35–36, NLT)

You are the one who faithfully watches over your child. It's you who is the safeguard. God wants to keep your child safe too. He's exceptional at watching over those He loves. Let your Father go to battle for your child and take a much-needed break. "The LORD will fight for you; you need only to be still." (Exodus 14:14, NIV). Keep in mind that there's never a time when you are the only one watching over your child.

Rest assured, God is passionately devoted to your child.

My prayer for today...

_____

_____

_____

_____

_____

_____

_____

_____

_____

_____

_____

Giving

And don't forget to do good and to share with those in need. These are the sacrifices that please God. (Hebrews 13:16, NLT)

If it is true that it is better to give than receive, then Amy knew this intuitively. We especially noticed this around the holidays. She was always trying to give her toys away. One Christmas she received an adorable baby doll. As soon as she opened that present, she took it to her sister Susan and gave it to her. Susan, of course, tried to give it back, but Amy just kept placing it in Susan's arms, getting upset that Susan wouldn't keep it.

We witnessed Amy's generosity at Easter too. We went to an Easter egg hunt at Hayes

Memorial. Each little child was given a basket for their eggs. As the kids found an egg, they would take it and put it in each other's baskets! Amy loved sharing her eggs with others and was delighted to drop an egg in a friend's basket.

Often we need help in our everyday lives. When we do, we can look to the One who has much to give. We can run to Him with our needs. "The LORD is a refuge for the oppressed, a stronghold in times of trouble. Those who know your name trust in you, for you, LORD, have never forsaken those who seek you." (Psalm 9:9–10, NIV). We are safe with God. We will feel His presence when we move closer to feel His support. "The LORD replied, "My Presence will go with you, and I will give you rest." (Exodus 33:14, NIV).

You have a lot on your plate right now, probably more than you feel you can handle. God wants to give you a break. Jesus says, "Take my yoke upon you and learn from me, for I am gentle and humble in heart, and you will find rest for your souls." (Matthew 11:29, NIV). Wouldn't you like to find some rest right about now? "The LORD is my shepherd, I lack nothing. He makes me lie down in green pastures, he leads me beside quiet waters, he refreshes my soul. He guides me along the right paths for his name's sake." (Psalm 23:1–3, NIV). Tonight, ask Jesus to lead you to a restful night.

> *Newsflash: God knows how to give good gifts to His children.*

My prayer for today...

_____

_____

_____

_____

_____

_____

_____

_____

_____

_____

_____

Closeness

But as for me, it is good to be near God. I have made the Sovereign LORD my refuge; I will tell of all your deeds. (Psalm 73:28, CEV)

Amy had difficulty going to sleep because of her labored breathing. One night when she was around eight years old, I lay beside her on the couch where she slept. While I watched her breathe, I prayed for her. Then I began to pray for myself as I realized how much guidance I needed to care for this beautiful child. I remembered what Jesus said when He went to heaven. He said He would send his Holy Spirit to guide and comfort us. I desperately wanted that in my life.

I began to pray that the Holy Spirit would be a daily part of my life. Raising Amy required more wisdom than I had, and I wanted all that God had to offer. As Amy slept beside me, I began to experience such a profound sense of peace and covering. It's hard to explain. However, in the core of my being I knew the Holy Spirit had come to be a part of my life in a new way, and from that night on I would never be the same. Jesus had done what He promised, and it was overwhelming.

We all need to feel God's closeness. Often the problems we encounter are too big for us. Facing them alone is a daunting task. It's good to know God moves closer during the hard times and continues to support us. "The LORD is close to the broken-hearted; he rescues those whose spirits are crushed." (Psalm 34:18, NLT). When the chips are down and you're wondering if you have what it takes to keep going, the Holy Spirit will bring you comfort.

Raising a child who has unique problems requires strength. The daily challenges you face require an endless supply of energy. Each day has more tasks than you can possibly do in a twenty-four hour period. That's why you need

Lessons from Amy

superhuman strength. That's why you rely on God. *"God arms me with strength, and he makes my way perfect. He makes me as surefooted as a deer, enabling me to stand on mountain heights. He trains my hands for battle; he strengthens my arm to draw a bronze bow."* (Psalm 18:32–34, NLT). You are the strongest when God is fighting with you.

Staying close to God keeps you from falling in the storms of life.

My prayer for today...

Uniqueness

"Before I formed you in the womb I knew you, before you were born I set you apart... (Jeremiah 1:5a, NIV)

Amy had a natural way of attracting others to her—even the bigger kids. She was loving and was always ready with a smile and a hug for each person she met. The older kids really loved this. They all wanted to play with her. She got piggyback rides around the yard and played hide-and-go-seek with her older brothers and their friends. They even invited her to play easy versions of tag or kickball.

October 27 was a special day in our house; it was Amy's birthday. She wasn't looking for a big production on her special day, Amy just wanted to be with the people she loved. She wanted to spend it with her family and her siblings' friends too. The teenage kids came over and brought her books and balloons. One boy always read to her and watched *Sesame Street* with her. They even took the time to color with her. Amy enjoyed simple pleasures.

God has a special heart for children. He's been thinking about them for a long time! "You watched me as I was being formed in utter seclusion, as I was woven together in the dark of the womb. You saw me before I was born. Every day of my life was recorded in your book. Every moment was laid out before a single day had passed." (Psalm 139:15–16, NLT). God watches over the little ones every day.

Your child is special too, despite the barriers in his or her life. God knows every little detail about your much-loved child. "Are not two sparrows sold for a penny? Yet not one of them will fall to the ground outside your Father's care. And even the very hairs of your head are all numbered. So don't be afraid; you are worth more than many sparrows." (Matthew 10:29–31, NIV).

God knows about all the big challenges you face each day, and He cares about the little problems too. Give your worries to Him, for His love for you is great and never-ending.

Remember, children are a special gift from God.

My prayer for today...

Peace

The LORD bless you and keep you; the LORD make his face shine on you and be gracious to you; the LORD turn his face toward you and give you peace. (Numbers 6:24–26, NIV)

In the quiet of the night, comfort unexpectedly appeared. In Amy's tenth year, she couldn't lie down because she was retaining fluid in her lungs that caused a continuous cough. I started to hold her against my chest all night so she could get some sleep. I'd listen to her breathing and put my cheek on her soft hair. At those times, my love for her exploded in my heart.

Late one night, my living room was so dark I couldn't see anything. My eyes searched and searched for any semblance of light. Finally, I was drawn to look up and saw a small beam of light beginning to shine over us. That's when I saw Amy and myself sitting at the bottom of a well. The light grew brighter and brighter, and a hand from heaven reached down, picked us up, and drew us towards the light. In the brightness I saw beauty all around us—trees, flowers, and green grass. Feeling securely held, I slept peacefully the rest of the night.

Nighttime shifts our focus to dark thoughts. That's when the worries and cares of the world begin to rest on our shoulders. They become a broken record that robs us of our rest and peace. God has a different plan for our nights. "Come to me, all of you who are weary and carry heavy burdens, and I will give you rest." (Matthew 11:28, NLT). When our thoughts are dark, we can be totally honest and simply say, "God, I need help from you tonight. Give me the peace you promised so I can turn off my thoughts and get some rest. Amen."

Lessons from Amy

*The child you're caring for needs you to be at your best. Getting a good night's rest will help you stay strong. God wants to take the night shift for you. Talk to Him in prayer right before you go to bed, and hand over everything that keeps you from sleeping well. He knows what to do with all your cares. Then you can confidently say, "In peace I will lie down and sleep, for you alone, L*ORD*, make me dwell in safety." (Psalm 4:8, NIV).*

Refuse to have another sleepless night. Give God your troubles and let Him bless you with His perfect peace.

My prayer for today...

Strength

You are my hiding place; you will protect me from trouble and surround me with songs of deliverance. (Psalm 32:7, NIV)

We didn't get any warning the day Amy left us. Her body was retaining fluid, so she had gained extra weight. Her low energy kept her on the couch all day. Although usually chatty, she couldn't talk much; the shortness of breath slowed her down. Amy was uncomfortable, and that made her restless. We tried to reposition her and rearranged her pillows, but our efforts were futile. I kept thinking that if she'd just go to sleep, she'd feel better tomorrow.

Later in the day, Bob sat behind her so she could lean on him. We all stayed close to her that day, wanting to give her what little comfort we could. Eventually, she couldn't keep her eyes open any longer. She leaned her head against her daddy and closed her eyes. I softly touched her cheek. I didn't even realize she'd left us until my son said from the stairway, "Mom, let her go. She's gone." Unbelievably, my baby had gone to heaven.

When days get tough for us, we need to find strength. We need a place to turn, and when we do, it needs to be towards Jesus. Let's not get lost by looking all over the place. Let's focus on the only One who can hold us up. "Let your eyes look straight ahead; fix your gaze directly before you. Give careful thought to the paths for your feet and be steadfast in all your ways. Do not turn to the right or the left." (Proverbs 4:25–27, NIV). Into the eyes of our Father is the place to look. Life is tough, but with God's backing, so are we.

A child with precise needs takes a lot of strength. You've been holding yourself together for a long time. But what if you could get some much-needed help? You can! There's a Father who has the power to keep you standing. "See, God has come to save me. I will trust in him and not be afraid. The LORD God is my strength and my song; he has given me victory." (Isaiah 12:2, NLT). God's angels are watching over you too. "For he will order his angels to protect you wherever you go." (Psalm 91:11, NLT). Take heart. Your Father has you completely covered!

Rest in the assurance that God has you surrounded.

My prayer for today...

_____

_____

_____

_____

_____

_____

_____

_____

_____

Sincerity

*Blessed are the pure in heart, for they
will see God. (Matthew 5:8, NIV)*

When Amy passed, I immediately went into our
bedroom to be alone. I needed to have a con-
versation with my Father, and it wasn't going to
be a quiet one. My raging emotions were out of
control, and I didn't want my family to witness
them. I got down on my knees and shouted,
"God, don't you know this is my daughter?" Did
He not understand what I was going through?
Did He even know my heart was breaking?

His answer was immediate, and it spoke
directly into my heart. "Don't you know that He
was my Son?" That's when I realized God knew
exactly what I was feeling, because He gave His

one and only Son to die on a cross for me. I literally fell to the floor. I begged His forgiveness and immediately felt His love surround me. Despite the difficulty of the day, a peace came over me in that moment. After a bit, I quietly went out to the living room and gave my girl one last hug.

Hardships drive us to our knees. Sometimes we cry out in anger, and other times we cry out in pain. Either way, God hears us and can handle all our emotions. He is not upset by how we approach Him. In fact, He wants us to come to Him sincerely, with open hearts. He plans to strengthen and build us up again. "Let us then approach God's throne of grace with confidence, so that we may receive mercy and find grace to help us in our time of need." (Hebrews 4:16, NIV). Where do we go when life gets unbearable? God is the answer to that question.

Raising a child who needs extra attention fills your life with uncertainty. When the problems are huge, solutions are hard to come by. But Jesus specializes in the impossible. When the odds are stacked against your child, go directly to Him. Jesus said, "Humanly speaking, it is impossible. But with God everything is possible." (Matthew

Lessons from Amy

19:26, NLT). Can you imagine that nothing is impossible with God? He can make things happen for you that you can't do on your own. Do you have too many problems today? Ask Him for the solutions you've been seeking.

The door to God's heart is always open. Walk through it today.

My prayer for today...

_____

_____

_____

_____

_____

_____

_____

_____

_____

_____

Hope

And I am certain that God, who began the good work within you, will continue his work until it is finally finished on the day when Christ Jesus returns. (Philippians 1:6, NLT)

The funeral for Amy was unexpectedly crowded. Our family and friends, her teachers and classmates from the School of Hope, and our kids' friends filled the church. It seemed everyone wanted one last goodbye. The older kids brought flowers and put stuffed animals in the casket. At the funeral home, the pastor spoke about coming to Jesus as a little child. He said we should come with sincerity and an open heart, just like Amy went into heaven.

As the funeral progressed, we sang her favorite songs. They reminded us of her innocence. "Jesus loves me, this I know, for the Bible tells me so." She also loved, "Here's my cup Lord, fill it up Lord." The songs were a fitting tribute to Amy's sweetness. That day, I really wanted to remind everyone not to take their children for granted, for they are a gift from God. I wanted people to never forget that truth.

Hopelessness can try to take hold of us when we are facing the storms of life. That's when we need to grasp the lifeline called faith. "I pray that God, the source of hope, will fill you completely with joy and peace because you trust in him. Then you will overflow with confident hope through the power of the Holy Spirit." (Romans 15:13, NLT). We must stand firm when trials are coming at us. God is working behind the scenes to assist us, so we can place our trust in Him.

It's challenging to hope today will be better than yesterday when your child is struggling. It might seem that things will never change, but that's just not true. In the Bible, many believed David was stuck, and he went from being a shepherd boy to a king! David said, "Many say about me, 'But you, LORD, are a shield around me, my glory, the One who lifts my head high. I call out to the LORD, and he answers me from his holy mountain. I lie down and sleep; I wake again, because the LORD sustains me.'" (Psalm 3:3–5, NIV). Here's good news: David's story is your story.

There's always a reason to hope.

My prayer for today...

Purpose

Let us not become weary in doing good, for at the proper time we will reap a harvest if we do not give up. (Galatians 6:9, NIV)

Bob knew immediately that I was going to struggle if I didn't find something to do. Taking care of Amy had been a full-time job. But what would I do now with all my time? Years ago, I had wanted to be a nurse, so Bob suggested I go into nurse's training. I thought I was too old to go back to school, but Susan and Bobby thought it was a good idea. Don wondered, "Why would you want to go back to school?" With most of the family's blessing, I decided to give it a try.

I must admit I had my doubts about it. After all those years, was this even possible? However, the thought of being able to help others drove me on. When I feared I wasn't good enough, my instructor was a great support. She said, "Calm down, everything is fine. I am satisfied with your work." To my complete surprise, at the end of the course I received the "Student of the Class" award. This was an unexpected but helpful confirmation.

We often feel inadequate to face the tasks before us. The problems seem so huge and we seem so small. But God can handle problems! He not only goes before us, He helps us get rid of the problems we are facing. "But be assured today that the LORD your God is the one who goes ahead of you like a devouring fire. He will destroy them; he will subdue them before you. And you will drive them out and annihilate them quickly, as the Lord has promised you." (Deuteronomy 9:3, NIV). Your problems are officially warned.

Taking care of your individual child is a full-time job. Problems arise that cause worry, and then each day becomes a chore to get through. That's when it's time to hand your worries over to the

One who can handle them easily. "Don't worry about anything; instead, pray about everything. Tell God what you need, and thank him for all he has done. Then you will experience God's peace, which exceeds anything we can understand. His peace will guard your hearts and minds as you live in Christ Jesus." (Philippians 4:6–7a, NLT). Place your tent near the campground of peace.

When your circumstances cause worry, trade the worry in for peace.

My prayer for today...

_____

_____

_____

_____

_____

_____

_____

_____

_____

Contentment

But godliness with contentment is great gain. (1 Timothy 6:6, NIV)

Being a nurse was fulfilling for me. I felt like I was able to make such an impact on people. There were opportunities to help patients every single day at the hospital. I helped with the expected duties of a nurse, but there were intangibles too. Sometimes people would ask me to pray with them or for them. I never would have been able to do that if I had been home each day. At the end of my fourth year, I was shocked to be given the "Nurse of the Year" award. I never would have dreamed something like that was possible for someone like me.

I was able to stay at the hospital for many years until it changed owners. During that time, it really felt like something good came out of my past challenges. This verse from the Bible became real to me, "And we know that in all things God works for the good of those who love him, who have been called according to his purpose." (Romans 8:28, NIV). I understood there was a bigger picture to my life, and it was still unfolding.

Standing on the promises of God is hard when our lives take an unexpected and unwanted turn. It's important to stay close to God in the trials of life as well as the celebrations. We need to discover the secret. "I know what it is to be in need, and I know what it is to have plenty. I have learned the secret of being content in any and every situation, whether well fed or hungry, whether living in plenty or in want. I can do all this through him who gives me strength." (Philippians 4:12–13, NIV). Who wouldn't want God's amazing strength?

You worry. You fret. You ponder what is best for your child. When your mind is spinning, you are thinking the way the world thinks. But when your mind is at peace, you are thinking like God.

He has a suggestion to get you from worry to peace. "Don't copy the behavior and customs of this world, but let God transform you into a new person by changing the way you think. Then you will learn to know God's will for you, which is good and pleasing and perfect." (Romans 12:2, NLT). God's thoughts are always better than our own.

God promises to give you the gift of peace. Will you accept it?

My prayer for today...

Understanding

*Praise be to the God and Father of
our Lord Jesus Christ, the Father of
compassion and the God of all comfort,
who comforts us in all our troubles, so
that we can comfort those in any trouble
with the comfort we ourselves receive from
God. (2 Corinthians 1:3–4, NIV)*

After I finished working at the hospital, God's
plans for my life continued to unfold. I was still
caregiving, but in a different way. I was able to
work as a home health care nurse. This meant I
helped patients after surgery during their recovery. I would visit them in their homes and see to

their care: taking temperatures, monitoring pain medications, and changing bandages. Often, they just needed a friend to talk with them.

Being in patients' homes really allowed me the chance to get to know them on a personal level. I loved every minute of it! There was one elderly patient who just liked having me there. I held her hand while we talked, and she had me pray with her. Another patient wanted me to sing hymns with her. Because music is such a universal language, she felt a sense of joy while we sang. I know I was there to help in their recovery, but my life became truly blessed because of them.

When trouble comes knocking at our door, we wish we didn't have to answer. Unfortunately, it seems to be able to find us no matter where we live. So, if we know trouble is going to find us, what should we do about it? Let's have God answer the door. "The blameless spend their days under the LORD's care, and their inheritance will endure forever. In times of disaster they will not wither; in days of famine they will enjoy plenty." (Psalm 37:18–19, NIV). We are safe with God.

Caring for and protecting your extraordinary child is a full-time job. You have too many decisions to make every day. You have many thoughts that make you worry. You have numerous needs that must be met. God wants to help in every part of your life: your decisions, your worries, and your needs. "And my God will meet all your needs according to the riches of his glory in Christ Jesus." (Philippians 4:19, NIV). What do you need today? Ask God for help.

God can do more than you could ever think or imagine.

My prayer for today...

_____

_____

_____

_____

_____

_____

_____

Understanding

Connections

When we get together, I want to encourage you in your faith, but I also want to be encouraged by yours. (Romans 1:12, NLT)

I never considered myself someone who could get up in front of a group of people and talk about my life. However, when the pastor asked me to share my testimony about our life with Amy, I agreed. He told me to speak from the heart. I realized that there could be mothers in the congregation who might need to hear my story. Perhaps hearing about Amy's life would bring them comfort. My message that day was clear: let God's love wash over you and carry you through every day of your life. His love will make all the difference.

There were other ways I was given the opportunity to talk about Amy. It happened one day when I had an eye appointment. Unbeknownst to me, she had conceived a Down's syndrome baby and knew some of Amy's story. That connected our hearts. She asked questions about Amy, and I could share that God supplied the strength I needed to raise our girl. I believe the eye doctor was comforted, knowing she had someone who understood not only her daily challenges but also what a special gift she was given in her child.

We are not meant to travel through this life alone. It's not "us against the world." We are created for relationship—connecting with people and connecting with God. It's in the togetherness that we are strong. No one wants to be standing in the trenches alone: we need a friend by our side. "Two people are better off than one, for they can help each other succeed. If one person falls, the other can reach out and help. But someone who falls alone is in real trouble." (Ecclesiastes 4:9–10, NLT).

Caring for the particular needs of your child can make you feel isolated. The world seems to go on around you as you are singularly focused on your child. But you're never alone in raising your child. God stays with you. "And be sure of this: I am with you always, even to the end of the age." (Matthew 28:20b, NLT). God will stay close to you; the tough days are no match for Him.

Take time to connect with the One who is always nearby.

My prayer for today...

_____

_____

_____

_____

_____

_____

_____

_____

_____

_____

_____

_____

Epilogue

So we don't look at the troubles we can see now; rather, we fix our gaze on things that cannot be seen. For the things we see now will soon be gone, but the things we cannot see will last forever. (2 Corinthians 4:18, NLT)

Amy's life transformed mine in ways that will remain with me for the rest of my life. Because of her, my joy in simple pleasures increased. Her delight and affection for people and animals caused me to look afresh at the world around me. Through her eyes, a world of possibilities opened to me. It was the little things that made her happy; everything became something to behold.

Looking at people the way God looks at them isn't always easy, but Amy did it every day. She accepted people as they were, not as she thought they should be. If you were on her radar, there was a good chance you would find a new friend. Her gentle nature was attractive and drew others in. I learned to be more patient with the faults of others, and serving others became a way of life.

I discovered an inner strength I didn't realize I had. Caring for Amy took every ounce of energy I had, so I had to dig deep to make it through those especially tough days. In that struggle, I discovered God's faithfulness and constant support while I cared for Amy. His continual guidance and wisdom were irreplaceable and never-ending. I needed His help to survive the many longs nights. Amy brought me closer to my heavenly Father.

After Amy's passing, I was able to find a new purpose. I found that caring for Amy's needs made me a better nurse. I learned to look at even the small details that made up a patient's care, so I could ease their burdens in a greater way. If a child was entrusted to my care, my attention

Lessons from Amy

and compassion increased exponentially. My heart would always be tuned to children.

As will happen, life moved on, and my children grew up. Bob and I stayed on the family farm. We have found peace in the house we shared with Amy. She is never far from our thoughts, and she lives forever in our hearts. "Three things will last forever—faith, hope, and love—and the greatest of these is love" (1 Corinthians 13:13, NLT).

In Memory

Amy Sue Binger

Given to us: October 27, 1968
Restored to Him: April 22, 1979

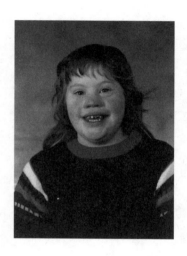

Lessons from Amy